A SOUND APPROACH

A SOUND APPROACH

*Phonemic English Methods with
Learning Aids and Study Helps*

Gene Miner

A SOUND APPROACH
PHONEMIC ENGLISH METHODS WITH LEARNING AIDS AND STUDY HELPS

iUniverse books may be ordered through booksellers or by contacting:

iUniverse
1663 Liberty Drive
Bloomington, IN 47403
www.iuniverse.com
844-349-9409

ISBN: 978-1-6632-3905-1 (sc)
ISBN: 978-1-6632-3904-4 (e)

Library of Congress Control Number: 2022907721

Print information available on the last page.

iUniverse rev. date: 04/27/2022

For Kermit W. (Kert) Dees

May 11,1910 - March 26, 2011

His genius created this work.

CONTENTS

FOREWORD

THIS Johnny CAN Read

Half a century ago Rudolf Flesch produced a wildly-popular book entitled "Why Johnny Can't Read". Its vitriolic attack on whole-word and other methods of teaching reading was in turn counter-attacked as over-simplified propaganda unsupported by research. Flesch and his detractors have joined the long train of profferers of methodologies which have provided at best partial answers to the vexing problem of learning to read a language which often doesn't look like it sounds. A new engine for this long train of methodologies is climbing its first hill, and we're beginning to hear "I think I can..."

The following is an account of a seven-year-old boy's experience with our system, the details of which are described in the ensuing document.

Our "Johnny" (not his real name) started his academic career by flunking first grade, and being dropped out of a remedial program the following summer. As one might expect, behavioral problems accompanied his inability to meet expectations in this forbidden, closed world of letters on a page.

The general procedure consisted of a series of sessions with the designer of our program focusing on rapport—and confidence—building, and introducing the content and procedures of the program. Between these sessions, Johnny was tutored and monitored in the use of program materials by his eleven-year-old sister at home. Most of

Johnny's program time was spent in unsupervised practice with the materials using a computer and other aids.

Observing some of the process develop, I became impressed that when Johnny learned that words written as they sound corresponded to what he already knew as a speaker, he became intensively involved, and eager to demonstrate his new reading skill. Our system always pairs its dependable phonemic spellings of words with their standard spellings, so that the learner is constantly exposed to the latter during practice. For Johnny, that connection has apparently been made because he seems increasingly comfortable with reading material written in Standard English.

Perhaps most dramatic has been Johnny's progress in school. Teacher reports have been progressively more encouraging, the latest ones placing him at the top of his class in reading and on the honor roll.

While we can't present this evidence as conclusive, as in a controlled experiment, we submit that the intervention clearly seems to have been associated with dramatic learning progress, and positive change in the life of this youngster. In one semester, going from flunking twice, to honor roll, poses the crux question: "How?"

Kenneth W. Carter, Ph.D. (Psychology)

PREFACE

Learning to read and write USA English is a nightmare of nonsense. Literacy in the English-speaking world doesn't start out as a nightmare. First communication steps begin early: neonates can recognize and respond to voices they have been exposed to in the womb.[1] Infants normally live in a rich verbal environment until that special day when their random/imitative vocalizations produce that eagerly-anticipated first word! With reinforcement from all sides, the baby/child adds words and begins to associate them with the objects and the actions they represent. By perhaps 18 months we hear two or more words spoken together, and before long we're hearing short meaningful sentences—sentences actually following language rules. Whether these grammatical outpourings spring from osmosis, an inborn grammatical capacity, or elsewhere, is an unsettled issue. Our point is that the normal, healthy human, exposed to a linguistic environment, seemingly effortlessly develops the ability to hear and understand, and to speak the language he/she is exposed to.

One would hope that this smooth progression would continue when the child is expected to learn to move beyond hearing/speaking to reading/writing, in school classrooms. And indeed speakers of some languages do seem to make this leap effortlessly and near-universally. But not so with English! Here it's a tough task for all, and a nightmare for many. The dimensions of the problem, which justify our use of the term nightmare, are appalling. Proportions of English-speakers unable

[1] http://www.beginbeforebirth.org/ in-the-womb/fetal-development The fetus begins to respond to sounds at about 20 weeks into the pregnancy

to read and write are far greater than those associated with virtually every other modern language. The various forms of dyslexia and other reading/writing-related problems appear to be far more prevalent with our language than with others which have been compared on that dimension.

So how can a language which some call the world's most expressive, and one which is being adopted worldwide at a rapid pace be so fraught with peril? The culprit is plain to see: SPELLING. The English repertoire of speech sounds, about 40 in number, is not represented simply and logically by written symbols, about 40 in number, but rather by something like 1100![2] In marshaling an army of foreign words to reinforce this most expressive language, our educators opted to retain, and create, exotic and archaic spellings, at the expense of accessibility and clear communication. Those of us who have mastered English tend to forget the magnitude of this expense charged to defenseless English-learners (of all ages).

Teachers of reading and writing struggle valiantly with this problem. The phonics vs. whole-language controversy is only one of the many battlegrounds characterized more by defeats than by victories. There seems little choice between the prodigious feats of sight-memory required by the latter, and the former's many rules which more often than not seem inapplicable.

Why, we must ask, do educators not remember and take advantage of the fact that children begin school equipped with a measure of literacy in English?! Must we essentially ignore that literacy, and immediately teach exotic spellings which confront kids with what amounts to a new language?

* * *

We offer a more humane and effective answer to the nightmare described above. Using 36 symbols composed of typeable letters and letter combinations (and the "Silent X Marker" to separate odd syllables) to represent the phoneme sounds of English, this system

---

[2] Kher, Unmesh. *Deconstructing Dyslexia: Blame It On The Written Word*. Time. March 26, 2001 Vol. 157 No. 12

immediately gives learners the tools to read and to write any English word they can hear and speak. After learning to vocalize the sounds represented by these 36 phoneme symbols, they are ready to read aloud any word spelled in these phoneme symbols. On any standard USA keyboard, they can also type any word they can say. Development of these skills is an immense accomplishment—tantamount to the whole task of learning to read and write a language which employs sensible (phonemic) spelling.

Because its spelling makes English essentially a bi-lingual language (the logical spelling described in the above paragraph, and the illogical spelling so characteristic of today's English), we forge a relationship between its phonemic spelling scheme and the mostly non-phonemic spelling scheme we are faced with today. We accomplish that by supplying the learner a 2-line presentation of written material, the top line with conventional spelling, and the bottom line with words spelled phonemically as described above. As the learner practices words with the familiar, comfortable phonemic spellings, he/she is directly presented with matched-sound words that have the conventional spellings that must be learned. Knowing the pronunciation of the strange-looking word in the upper line and frequently recognizing it as a friend from one's spoken vocabulary constitute a significant head start in mastering the strange spelling taught in schools.

Though individual learning styles and the mechanisms employed vary, we are certain that experiencing the two forms together forges a connection which facilitates recognition of the most exotically-spelled words.

CHAPTER 1

Learning Can Be Made Easier

Generally, learning can be made easier. Specifically, essential learning can be made easier in language, mathematics and physical science. Language is essential to modern human communication. Making language learning easier must come first. Still more specifically, making learning USA English easier is our primary short-term objective.

We make learning USA English easier by providing the essential information, methods and tools that are necessary but either do not yet exist or are unavailable in learning environments.

Literacy

We consider automatic processes or those accomplished without conscious effort to be functions of the brain. We call actions that require learning or conscious effort functions of the mind. These distinctions are important in any consideration of literacy.

Until humans learned to inscribe symbols that could be encoded to represent sounds, literacy consisted primarily of the spoken language. The two components of early spoken-language literacy are Auditing and Speaking. Auditing is the process of hearing with understanding. Speaking is the process of vocalizing with meaning. Human beings are predisposed to Auditing and Speaking not only through the

1

development of the ear and the vocal chords, but at the same time through the development of the processing center–the brain. Auditing and Speaking are phenomena of the brain (these processes happen without conscious effort). The healthy pre-schooler picks up words from those around her/him: parents, siblings, grandparents, baby sitters and others. Our healthy pre-schooler is a child who has, after correction, normal vision, normal hearing and no significant speech impediments. By the time the child is ready to enter pre-school, she/he has learned to converse sensibly with both peers and adults. It is critically important for parents and teachers to recognize that healthy pre-schoolers have already learned to communicate in their native language: They hear with understanding (Auditing) and vocalize with meaning, including word order and sentences (Speaking). We characterize a child's auditing and speaking in English as "KidsEnglish".

The development of symbols that could be encoded to represent sounds introduced the concepts of Reading and Writing. Reading is the process of recognizing and interpreting the meaning of words, word groups and accompanying effects such as images and marks that make up printed text.

The successful reader can say aloud, without memorization, printed text (appropriate to her/his level of learning) with consistent flow, clear speech, appropriate emphasis, and understanding. Writing is the process of organizing and displaying the words and word groups and accompanying effects such as images and marks that make up printed text. These two relative newcomers to literacy have become so popular that the importance of Auditing and Speaking has been all but ignored. Auditing and Speaking are still essentials of literacy and are still the domain of the brain. Human beings are not predisposed to Reading and Writing. Reading text requires auditing from symbols rather than sounds (one must hear with her/his eyes). Writing text requires converting speaking into symbols (one must see with her/his ears). Reading and Writing are human inventions and, as such, are phenomena of the mind (these processes do not happen without conscious effort).

BiLingual English

Because the conscious efforts necessary to learn reading and writing USA English are not closely related to the unconscious processes of learning auditing and speaking, we have characterized USA English as "BiLingual". By this term we refer to the regrettable gulf between the sounds of Auditing-Speaking and the symbols of Reading-Writing. Words don't look like they sound or sound like they look. The sounds of Auditing-Speaking are called "phoneme sounds" and the symbols of Reading-Writing are called "phoneme symbols".

USA English uses approximately 40 phoneme sounds. Dictionary publishers and linguists have created phoneme symbols that represent phoneme sounds. Written words are supposed to be made up of phoneme symbols just as spoken words are made up of phoneme sounds. A dictionary's phoneme symbols are listed in its pronunciation guide. Also, in most dictionaries the phoneme symbols of a listed word usually follow the word in parentheses. These symbols are not available for general use by the public because not all of them can be typed on standard keyboards. Consequently teachers have been forced to rely on alphabetic symbols alone for teaching reading and writing. Historically so-called phonemic constructions have evolved haphazardly through changes, primarily in the usage of vowels, in the construction of English words. Now there are reportedly more than 1,000 different alphabetic constructions for USA English phoneme symbols. Table 1-1 illustrates a variety of spellings for each phoneme vowel sound:

Table 1-1 A few common spellings for each phoneme vowel sound.

RHD is the abbreviation for Random House Dictionary. The symbol in parentheses is RHD's phoneme symbol. The block-letter symbol following the equal sign is our phoneme symbol.				
RHD (a) = A	RHD (e) = E	RHD (i) = I	RHD (o) = O	RHD (u) = U
a hat	e ebb	I If	o box	u pup
a'a ma'am	a any	a damage	a wander	o son
ag diaphragm	ae aesthete	E England	ach yacht	oe does
ai plaid	ai said	ee been	au astronaut	oo blood
al half	ay says	ei counterfeit	eau bureaucracy	ou trouble
au laugh	ea leather	ia carriage	ou cough	
	eg phlegm	ie sieve		
	ei heifer	o women		
		u business		
		y sympathetic		
RHD (~) = AE	RHD (') = EE	RHD (§) = IE	RHD (Ç) = OE	RHD (ÇÇ) = UE
a ate	ee keep	i...e ice	o lo	oo ooze
ag champagne	ae Caesar	ai faille	au mauve	eu maneuver
ai rain	ay quay	ais aisle	eau beau	ew grew
aig arraign	e equal	ay aye	eo yeoman	ieu lieu
au gauge	ea team	ei stein	ew sew	o move
ay ray	ei receive	eigh height	o...e rote	oe canoe
e suede	eip receipt	eye eye	oa road	ou troupe
ea steak	eo people	ie pie	oe toe	u...e rule
ee matinee	ey key	igh high	oh oh	ue flue
ei veil	i machine	is island	ol yolk	ui suit
eig feign	ie field	uy buy	oo brooch	
eigh sleigh	oe amoeba	y sky		
ey obey	y city	ye lye		

This table is excerpted from *Random House Webster's Unabridged Dictionary v3.0* (p. xxxviii).

We characterize the teaching of reading and writing of English in alphabetic symbols only as "SchoolEnglish". SchoolEnglish ignores the child's language(Brain) and attempts to force the brain to translate the written symbols of SchoolEnglish (Mind) directly into the spoken sounds of KidsEnglish (Brain).

We characterize this forced translation process as "Standard English". Symbols that don't match sounds don't make sense. It is no wonder if the brain resists. The brain's resistance to learning symbols that don't match sounds results in slowness, if not actual refusal, to learn; loss of confidence; and even in several forms of Dyslexia.

CHAPTER 2

Phonemic English

Learning Phonemic Awareness

In Chapter 1 of Phonemic Awareness in Young Children, a Classroom Curriculum, Marilyn Jager Adams et al say "Before children can make any sense of the alphabetic principle, they must understand that those sounds that are paired with the letters are one and the same as the sounds of speech."[3] This statement is generally false because it misleads both educators and learners into thinking that the letters of the standard USA English alphabet represent sounds in some sensible, consistent fashion. The learner could spend the rest of her/his life trying to make sense of the relationship between speech sounds and the letters of the USA English alphabet with great frustration and little success. The fact is that the letters of the USA English alphabet do not represent sounds in any sensible or consistent fashion. Although those letters that are supposed to represent consonant sounds are fairly consistent, those that are supposed to represent vowel sounds are far from consistent. Each letter represents a significant number of

---

[3] Adams, Marilyn J., Barbara R. Foorman, Ingvar Lundberg, and Terri Beeler. 1998. Phonemic Awareness in Young Children, a Classroom Curriculum. Baltimore. Paul H. Brookes Publishing Co.

different vowel sounds and a single vowel sound is often represented by several different letters.[4]

Adams et al go on to define phonemes as "...the small units of speech that correspond to letters of an alphabetic writing system". If one accepts such a correspondence, then a proper definition of phonemes is the small units of speech that correspond to the symbols of a phonemic alphabet writing system. The alphabet of USA English is not a phonemic alphabet. There is no sensible correspondence between its letters and USA English phonemes.

It is just this lack of correspondence between the alphabet of USA English and the phonemes of USA English that makes phonemic awareness so difficult for educators to teach and to measure and so difficult for children to learn. Adams et al state "The challenge, therefore, is to find ways to get children to notice the phonemes, to discover their existence and separability." The way to get children to notice the phonemes is to teach phonemes. On phoneme sounds, the authors further state "...developing readers must learn to separate these sounds, one from another, and to categorize them in a way that permits understanding of how words are spelled". We agree, but educators are not provided the tools to use, either for themselves or to pass on to these developing readers. The dilemma is how to foster phonemic awareness without proper tools.

The Phonemic Alphabet

We have selected, or developed, from the myriad of phonemic constructions in use today 36 essential, sensible, easily recognizable, consistent, typeable, phoneme symbols to represent the phoneme sounds common to KidsEnglish and Standard English. This set of 36 phoneme symbols is called the "Phonemic Alphabet". Using our Phonemic Alphabet to represent these phoneme sounds is characterized as "Phonemic English". The Phonemic Alphabet is presented with keywords in Table 2-1:

---

[4] Kher, Unmesh. Deconstructing Dyslexia: Blame It On The Written Word. Time. March 26, 2001 Vol. 157 No. 12.

Table 2-1. The Phonemic Alphabet.

(5) 1-Letter Vowel Symbols:	(6) 2-Letter Vowel Symbols:	(18) 1-Letter Consonant Symbols:		(7) 2-Letter Consonant Symbols:
A PAP	AE TAEK\take	B BAD	N NOT	CH CHIN (CH=T+SH)
E PEP	EE TEETH	D DAD	P POT	SH SHIN
I PIP	IE TIE	F FAD	R ROT	TH THIN
O POP	OE TOE	G GOT	S SAT	TZ TZEN\then
U PUP	UE TRUE	H HOT	T TAT	WH WHEN (WH=H+W)
	UU TUUK\took	J JOT (J=D+ZH)	V VAT	ZH AZHUR\azure
		K KIT	W WET	NG SING
		L LIT	Y YET	
		M MET	Z ZAP	

Note that a Phonemic English keyword that doesn't match its equivalent Standard English word is followed by "\" and the equivalent Standard English word. Note also that j, ch and wh are not primary phoneme symbols, but represent blends of primary phoneme symbols.

The Silent X Marker

Our Silent X Marker is used to indicate breaks between adjacent characters within words as shown in Table 2-2:

Table 2-2. The Silent X Marker is used to show separations.

Example:	Phonemic English:	Standard English American Heritage Dictionary:
coerce	KOEXURS	co·erce
defer	DIXFUR	de·fer
differ	DIFXUR	dif·fer
geranium	JUXRAEXNEEXUM	ge·ra·ni·um

Although it is not necessary to use the Silent X Marker with most words, the Silent X Marker is essential to separate adjacent vowels, as in KOEXURS and JURAENEEXUM, and to indicate the location of a slight pause in pronunciation, as in DIXFUR and DIFXUR. The

Silent X Marker can also be used to indicate the location of a slight pause in pronunciation in words that have more than two syllables as in JURAEXNEEXUM. If you want to use the Silent X Marker as a syllable separator and also to indicate the location of a slight pause in pronunciation, add an additional Silent X Marker as in JUXRAEXXNEEXUM. There is no sound associated with the Silent X Marker.

Other Diacritically Marked Vowels

In addition to developing the 36 typeable symbols, we provide the means to eliminate diacritic markings from other marked vowels. Examples are shown in Table 2-3:

Table 2-3. Method of eliminating diacritic markings.

Standard English American Heritage Dictionary:	Phonemic English:	Phonemic TheaterEnglish: (Not Recommended for Kids)
ar dare dâr	AER DAER\dare	AEXUR DAEXUR
ar far fär	OR FOR\far	
er here hîr	EER HEER\here	EEXUR HEEXUR
ir pier pîr	EER PEER\pier	EEXUR PEEXUR
or for fôr	OER FOER\for	OEXUR FOEXUR
ur urge ûrj	UR URJ\urge	UXUR UXURJ

Note that a Phonemic English keyword that doesn't match its equivalent Standard English word is followed by "\" and the equivalent Standard English word. Note also the use of the Silent X Marker in the Phonemic TheaterEnglish examples.

CHAPTER 3

Phoneme Symbols

Comparison of our Phoneme Symbols and the American Heritage Dictionary's Phoneme Symbols

Consonant Phoneme Symbols

Table 3-1. Comparison of our consonant phoneme symbols and the American Heritage Dictionary's consonant phoneme symbols with keywords.

Phonemic English Phoneme Symbol:	American Heritage Dictionary Phoneme Symbol:	Phonemic English Phoneme Symbol:	American Heritage Dictionary Phoneme Symbol:
B BAD	b	S SAT	s
D DAD	d	T TAT	t
F FAD	f	V VAT	v
G GOT	g	W WET	w
H HOT	h	Y YET	y
J JOT	j	Z ZAP	z
K KIT	k	CH CHIN	ch
L LIT	l	SH SHIN	sh
M MET	m	TH THIN	th
N NOT	n	TZ TZEN	tz

Phonemic English Phoneme Symbol:	American Heritage Dictionary Phoneme Symbol:	Phonemic English Phoneme Symbol:	American Heritage Dictionary Phoneme Symbol:
P POT	p	WH WHEN	wh
R ROT	r	ZH AZHUR\azure	zh
		NG SING	ng

Vowel Phoneme Symbols

Comparison of our **TYPEABLE** vowel phoneme symbols and the American Heritage Dictionary's vowel phoneme symbols with keywords:

Table 3-2. Comparison of our vowel phoneme symbols and the American Heritage Dictionary's vowel phoneme symbols.

Phonemic English Phoneme Symbol:	American Heritage Dictionary Phoneme Symbol:	Phonemic English Phoneme Symbol:	American Heritage Dictionary Phoneme Symbol:
A PAP	pap	O FOTZUR\father	father (ä=O)
E PEP	pep	A DAR\dare	dare (â=A)
I PIP	pip	EE PEER\pier	pier (î=EE)
O POP	pop	OE OERDUR\order	order (ô=OE)
U PUP	pup	U URJ\urge	urge (û=U)
AE TAEK\take	take	U SURKUS\circus	circus
EE TEETH	teeth		
IE TIE	tie		
OE TOE	toe		
UE TRUE	true		
UU TUUK\took	took (=UU)		

Note that a Phonemic English keyword that doesn't match its equivalent Standard English word is followed by "\" and the equivalent Standard English word.

Vowel Families

There are many different characterizations of "vowel families"—short vowel families, long vowel families, irregular vowel families and so on. There are also different characterizations within these vowel families. Most are oriented toward how words look, not how words sound.

We characterize vowel families by sound first. The vowel families are then arranged by how they look as shown in Table 3-3:

Table 3-3. How our vowel families are arranged.

Family:	1-Letter Vowel Symbols:	2-Letter Vowel Symbols:
a	A	AE
e	E	EE
i	I	IE
o	O	OE
u	U	UE, UU

CHAPTER 4

Build on What Kids Already Know

By the time they reach kindergarten, most children have been exposed to the alphabet and numerals (they have already learned their ABCs and Numbers). Children are seldom given the opportunity to learn the **names** of the letters of the alphabet and the **names** of the numerals. Now allow them to learn not only the **names** of the letters of the alphabet and the **names** of the numerals but also the **names** of the phonemes.

Phonemic English Names of the Letters of the Alphabet

Table 4-1 shows Phonemic English names of the letters of the alphabet:

Table 4-1. Our Phonemic English names of the letters of the alphabet.

Letter:	Phonemic English Name:	Letter	Phonemic English Name:
a	AE	n	EN
b	BEE	o	OE
c	SEE	p	PEE
d	DEE	q	KYUE
e	EE	r	OR

Letter:	Phonemic English Name:	Letter	Phonemic English Name:
f	EF	s	ES
g	JEE	t	TEE
h	AECH	u	YUE
i	IE	v	VEE
j	JAE	w	DUBULYUE
k	KAE	x	EKS
l	EL	y	WIE
m	EM	z	ZEE

Phonemic English Names of the Numerals

Table 4-2 shows Phonemic English names of the numerals:

Table 4-2. Our Phonemic English names of the numerals.

Numeral:	Phonemic English Name:	Numeral	Phonemic English Name:
0	ZIROE	5	FIEV
1	WUN	6	SIKS
2	TUE	7	SEVUN
3	THREE	8	AET
4	FOER	9	NIEN

Phonemic English Names of the Phonemes

One reason phonemes are not taught is that phoneme symbols are not commonly **named** as are, for example, the letters of the alphabet. Without **names** phoneme symbols are difficult to think and talk about as well as to remember.

Full phonemic awareness requires that we be able to talk about phoneme symbols in a way similar to the way that we talk about the letters of the alphabet. As we learn our ABC's, we are actually learning the names of the letters in the English alphabet. Because phoneme symbols are very different from letters, we need to be able to refer to them by their own names, and not by the alphabet symbols they're comprised of. We have created names for the phoneme symbols of our phonemic alphabet according to the following criteria:

- No phoneme symbol name will be the same as a letter name.
- Every phoneme symbol name will be spelled with letters of the alphabet (no special or untypeable symbols).
- Every phoneme symbol will have a name that can can be pronounced when read.

Our first vowel phoneme sound is represented by the letter "A", but as we've shown, that letter name is not useful for our phonemic purposes. Our phonemic alphabet assigns the letter "A" to the vowel sound in words like "at". So the name for our symbol "A" is "phoneme symbol A" or "phoneme A" (A as in PAP). In spoken form, "phoneme symbol A" or even "phoneme A" (Careful! Don't pronounce "A" like the alphabet letter.) is handy enough, but in written form, using "phoneme symbol" or "phoneme" before each symbol could become cumbersome. So we simplify our phoneme symbol names by following the symbol for each vowel sound with the letter "K". Hence: "AK" is the name of our first vowel phoneme symbol.

Table 4-3 shows Phonemic English names of our 11 Vowel Phoneme Symbols:

Table 4-3. Our Phonemic English names of the 11 Vowel Phoneme Symbols.

Phoneme Symbol:	Phonemic English Name:	Phoneme Symbol:	Phonemic English Name:
A	AK	AE	AEK
E	EK	EE	EEK
I	IK	IE	IEK
O	OK	OE	OEK
U	UK	UE	UEK
		UU	UUK

Our first consonant phoneme sound is represented by the letter "B". However, no consonant can be pronounced without a supporting vowel sound. So we add the short vowel sound "U" as in "PUP". Hence, our first consonant phoneme symbol's name is "phoneme symbol B", "phoneme B", or "BU".

Table 4-4 shows Phonemic English names of our 25 Consonant Phoneme Symbols:

**Table 4-4. Our Phonemic English names of the
25 Consonant Phoneme Symbols.**

Phoneme Symbol:	Phonemic English Name:	Phoneme Symbol:	Phonemic English Name:
B	BU	S	SU
D	DU	T	TU
F	FU	V	VU
G	GU	W	WU
H	HU	Y	YU
J	JU	Z	ZU
K	KU	CH	CHU
L	LU	SH	SHU
M	MU	TH	THU
N	NU	TZ	TZU
P	PU	WH	WHU
R	RU	ZH	ZHU
		NG	NGU

CHAPTER 5

Aren't Phonemes and Letters the Same Thing?

Phonemes and Letters Are Not the Same Thing

Our phoneme symbols are spelled with letters of the alphabet, but phoneme symbols and letters are not the same thing. Alphabet letters are for spelling. Phoneme symbols are for pronouncing. Table 5-1 shows a comparison of our phoneme symbols with alphabet letters:

Table 5-1. A comparison of our phoneme symbols and alphabet letters including phoneme symbol names and letter names.

Phoneme Symbol:	Phoneme Symbol Name:	Spelled with Letter(s):	Letter Name(s):
A	AK	a	AE
E	EK	e	EE
I	IK	i	IE
O	OK	o	OE
U	UK	u	YUE
AE	AEK	a, e	AE, EE
EE	EEK	e, e	EE, EE
IE	IEK	i, e	IE, EE
OE	OEK	o, e	OE, EE
UE	UEK	u, e	YUE, EE

Phoneme Symbol:	Phoneme Symbol Name:	Spelled with Letter(s):	Letter Name(s):
UU	UUK	u, u	YUE, YUE
B	BU	b	BEE
D	DU	d	DEE
F	FU	f	EF
G	GU	g	GEE
H	HU	h	AECH
J	JU	j	JAE
K	KU	k	KAE
L	LU	l	EL
M	MU	m	EM
N	NU	n	EN
P	PU	p	PEE
R	RU	r	OR
S	SU	s	ES
T	TU	t	TEE
V	VU	v	VEE
W	WU	w	DUBULYUE
Y	YU	y	WIE
Z	ZU	z	ZEE
CH	CHU	c, h	SEE, AECH
SH	SHU	s, h	ES, AECH
TH	THU	t, h	TEE, AECH
TZ	TZU	t, z	TEE, ZEE
WH	WHU	w, h	DUBULYUE, AECH
ZH	ZHU	z, h	ZEE, AECH
NG	NGU	n, g	EN, GEE

Decoding USA English Words

Written language is a code. A code is valid only to the extent that it can be coded (encryption) and decoded (decryption). What is written must represent what is spoken to facilitate translation to speech; what is spoken must be capable of translation to writing. Every code requires a two-way key for both encryption and decryption. To translate smoothly between writing and speech and between speech and writing requires a two-way key. Our typeable phoneme symbols provide that key.

Dictionary publishers and linguists have created phoneme symbols that represent phoneme sounds. A dictionary's phoneme symbols are listed in its pronunciation guide. Also, in most dictionaries the phoneme symbols of a listed word usually follow the word in parentheses. The key used by dictionary publishers and linguists is implicit. These symbols can not be used by the public as a key for coding and decoding because not all of them can be typed on standard keyboards. Because there is no explicit key, teachers have been forced to rely on alphabetic symbols alone for teaching reading and writing. Historically so-called phonemic constructions have evolved haphazardly through changes, primarily in the usage of vowels, in the construction of English words.

There are too many alphabetical spellings for the 35 to 40 phoneme sounds that make up the spoken English language. Time reporter Unmesh Kher asserts that there are more than 1,100 different alphabetical spellings of USA English phoneme symbols.[5]

By the time most children enter kindergarten, they have accumulated a sizeable vocabulary of words that they can pronounce properly. This vocabulary can be built on by letting these children see what their words look like, how the typewritten words can be decoded, and how the typewritten words can be sounded out.

Our set of symbols for decoding phonemes, blends, syllables, and words, makes Phonemic English words readily decodeable. Our set of symbols for decoding Phonemic English words separates from large to small:

word(), syllable ('), blend (,), and phoneme (.).

A space, (), represents the spacing between words.
An apostrophe, ('), represents the break between syllables.

---

[5] Kher, Unmesh. *Deconstructing Dyslexia: Blame It On The Written Word*. Time. March 26, 2001 Vol. 157 No. 12

A comma, (,), represents the separation of phonemes within blends,
A period, (.), represents the separation of individual phonemes.

The following are examples of decoding the word "consonant":

Spell in our typeable phoneme symbols: KONSUNUNT
Separate phonemes only: K.O.N.S.U.N.U.N.T
Separate syllables only: KON'SU'NUNT
Separate consonant blends only: KONSUNUN,T
Separate vowel-consonant blends only: K,O,NS,UN,U,NT
Separate phonemes, consonant blends and syllables:
K.O.N'S.U'N.U.N,T
Separate vowel-consonant blends, consonant blends and syllables:
K,O,N'S,U'N,U,N,T

Table 5-2 illustrates the use of these symbols for decoding
Phonemic English words:

Table 5-2. Examples of our symbols for decoding Phonemic
English words with sounding out and pronunciation.

Phonemic English Word:	Decoded Phonemic English Word:	Phonemic English Word Sounded Out:	Phonemic English Word Pronounced:
TZU\the	TZ.U	TZU.UK	TZU
AND	A.N,D	AK.NU,DU	AND
UTZUR\other	U.TZ'U.R	UK.TZU'.UK.RU	UTZUR
UNUTZUR\another	U'N.U.TZ'U.R	UK'NU.UK.TZU'.UK.RU	UNUTZUR
DIFURUNT\different	D.I.F'U.R'U.N,T	DU.IK.FU'UK.RU'UK.NU,TU	DIFURUNT
BURD\bird SONG	B.U.R,D S.O.NG	BU.UK.RU,DU SU.OK.NGU	BURD SONG

Note that we have taken advantage of the **names** of the phonemes
to assist sounding out (see Appendix III). As the **names** are sounded
out, gradually drop the "K" and "U" suffixes to finish pronouncing the
complete word.

CHAPTER 6

The TwoLine Method

Derivation of the TwoLine Method

We bring the dictionary's phonemic spelling and the dictionary's pronunciation of words to printed text. The American Heritage Dictionary, for example, lists the following for the word "connection":

con · nec · tion (kə-nĕk′shən)

In Phonemic English this entry would appear as follows:

KUNEKSHUN (K.U′N.E.K′SH.U.N)

Listing the word "connection" with its Phonemic English entry gives:

connection KUNEKSHUN (K.U′N.E.K′SH.U.N)

Arranging these examples one above the other produces:

connection
KUNEKSHUN (K.U′N.E.K′SH.U.N)
con · nec · tion (kə-nĕk′shən)

Eliminating the bottom line (some phonemes not typeable) and the decoded portion of the second line results in the TwoLine Method:

connection
KUNEKSHUN

Translating BiLingual English

Our TwoLine Method of translation between Phonemic English and Standard English consists of placing a series of words such as a phrase, sentence, paragraph or a complete work such as a poem or nursery rhyme in two lines one above the other. One line is Standard English, the other line is Phonemic English. Because Phonemic English is primary, we place the Phonemic English line below the Standard English line. The lines are arranged so that equivalent words are aligned vertically as shown in the example below:

Jack	Sprat	could	eat	no	fat,	<== Standard English
JAK	SPRAT	KUUD	EET	NOE	FAT,	<== Phonemic English

his	wife	could	eat	no	lean,
HIZ	WIEF	KUUD	EET	NOE	LEEN,

and	so	between	them	both,	you	see,
AND	SOE	BITWEEN	TZEM	BOETH,	YUE	SEE,

they	licked	the	platter	clean.
TZAE	LIKT	TZU	PLATUR	KLEEN.

The **Phonemic English** line **guides** the **pronunciation** of each word. Until there are dictionaries that provide the Phonemic English spelling of each word, the **Standard English** line **guides** access to the dictionary for the **meaning** of each word.

Spelling

Standard English words are spelled by naming the letters they contain. Phonemic English words are spelled by naming the phoneme symbols they contain. Consider the word "apple".

Standard English: **apple**

Phonemic English: **APUL**

Standard English Spelling: **AE-PEE-PEE-EL-EE** ==> **apple**

Phonemic English Spelling: **AK-PU-UK-LU** ==> **APUL**

The following phrase illustrates the strength of Phonemic English spelling compared to Standard English spelling:

Standard English Spelling:

I thought about you

IE TEE-AECH-OE-YUE-JEE-AECH-TEE AE-BEE-OE-YUE-TEE WIE-OE-YUE

Phonemic English Spelling:

IE THOT UBAUT YUE

IEK THU-OK-TU UK-BU-AK-UK-TU YU-UEK

Note that spelling Phonemic English words by naming the phoneme symbols they contain is a form of decoding.

Since our phoneme symbols are spelled with alphabetic characters, Phonemic English words can also be spelled by naming the letters they contain. **IE THOT UBAUT YUE** can be spelled:

IE TEE-AECH-OE-TEE YUE-BEE-AE-YUE-TEE WIE-YUE-EE

CHAPTER 7

The ThreeLine Method

English As a Second Language

Our TwoLine Method of translation between Phonemic English and Standard English is readily adaptable for translating between a non-English language and English. This method consists of placing a third line of words below the first two lines. The top line is Standard English, the second line is Phonemic English and the third line is the language being translated. The lines are arranged so that words that translate directly are aligned vertically and words that do not translate directly are arranged as **phrases** that are aligned vertically and **convey** the **meaning** as shown in the example below:

Jack	Sprat	could eat no	fat,	<== Standard English
JAK	SPRAT	KUUD EET NOE	FAT,	<== Phonemic English
Jack	Sprat	no podía comer	grasa,	<== Latino/Spanish

his	wife	could eat no	lean,
HIZ	WIEF	KUUD EET NOE	LEEN,
su	esposa	no podía comer	sin grasa,

and so	between	them both,	you	see,
AND SOE	BITWEEN	TZEM BOETH,	YUE	SEE,
entonces	entre	ellos,	usted	comprende,

they	licked	the	platter	clean.
TZAE	LIKT	TZU	PLATUR	KLEEN.
ellos	lamieron	el	plato	limpio.

The Phonemic English line guides the pronunciation of each word. Until there are dictionaries that provide the phonemic spelling of each word, the **Standard English** line **guides** access to the dictionary for the **meaning** of each word.

When a word or phrase does not translate directly and there is no equivalent word or phrase, the lines are arranged so that the words or phrases that do not translate directly are aligned vertically and the **non-translatable** words or phrases are **underlined** as shown in the example below:

Old	King	Cole	was	a	merry	old soul	<== Standard English
OELD	KING	KOEL	WUZ	U	MEREE	OELD SOEL	<== Phonemic English
El viejo	rey	Cole	era	una	alegre	alma vieja	<== Latino/Spanish

and		a		merry	old soul	was he
AND		U		MEREE	OELD SOEL	WUZ HEE
y		una		alegre	alma vieja	el era

he	called for	his	pipe,	
HEE	KOLD FOER	HIZ	PIEP,	
el	<u>pidió</u>	su	pipa,	<== underlined indicates no direct translation

and	he	called for	his	bowl,	
AND	HEE	KOLD FOER	HIZ	BOEL,	
y	el	<u>pidió</u>	su	tazón,	<== underlined indicates no direct translation

and	he	called for	his	fiddlers three.
AND	HEE	KOLD FOER	HIZ	FIDLURZ THREE.
y	el	llamó a	sus	tres violinistas.

Our method for introducing English as a second language requires first that the person assisting the learner be sufficiently fluent in both languages to be able to communicate sensibly in both. Our second requirement is that the person assisting the learner know which English phoneme sounds must be learned and which learner's phoneme sounds must be dropped in order for the learner to be able to pronounce English words using English phoneme sounds.

CHAPTER 8

Access to the Dictionary

Use a Talking Dictionary

A **talking dictionary** is **essential** as a standard for clear, third-party **pronunciation** of USA English words as well as for providing other dictionary functions such as definitions and thesaurus. There are several talking dictionaries available free online that provide pronunciation of USA English words. In addition to pronunciation, some versions provide a history list that is especially useful for setting up hearing and speaking drills. Two examples are Merriam-Webster (www.merriam-webster.com) and The Free Dictionary (www. thefreedictionary.com).

Keyboard

A **talking dictionary** is a **computer program** that provides easy, quick **access** to words for **pronunciation** and **meaning**. Every USA English learner needs such access as part of the process of learning to read. To take advantage of this easy, quick access to words, the learner must have access to and be able to use a **computer-type keyboard**.

As technology progresses in the 21st century, the **computer-type keyboard** with keycaps that display letters, numerals, characters, and other functions is evolving as the **universal translator** for all languages.

The user who is equipped with **typeable phoneme symbols** that consistently represent phoneme sounds has a **powerful advantage** in making use of this **invaluable tool**.

Caps Lock On

The first thing one encounters when using common keyboards is that on most keyboards all of the key-cap letters are shown upper-case only, i.e. as block letters. However, when someone new to the keyboard tries to type, the typed letters appear on the screen as lower-case only. What a dirty trick! To circumvent this problem we strongly recommend that every learner working in **Phonemic English** type with **Caps Lock on**. The typed letters appearing on the screen will look like the the key-cap letters on the keyboard. Typing with Caps Lock on creates a **one-to-one relationship** between the **keyboard** and the **screen** that will **enhance** rather than undermine the learner's **confidence**. This one-to-one relationship will add to the **one-to-one relationship** that exists between **Phonemic Englsih typed** words and **pronounc**ed words.

CHAPTER 9

LUUKS LIEK, SAUNDZ LIEK
[Looks Like, Sounds Like]

TZIS CHAPTUR IZ RITUN IN **BIE-LINGGWUL INGXGLISH** WITH FUNEEMIK INGXGLISH PRIEMEREE. STANDURD INGXGLISH IS SHOEN IN SKWAER BRAKITS []. [This chapter is written in **Bi-Lingual English** with Phonemic English primary. Standard English is shown in square brackets [].]

WITH STANDURD INGXGLISH U SIMPUL WURD LIEK "a" KAN BEE PRUNAUNST KUREKTLEE AZ A, AE OR U. [With Standard English a simple word like "a" can be pronounced correctly as A, AE or U.] WITH FUNEEMIK INGXGLISH NOE WURDZ THAT SOUND DIFURUNTLEE KAN HAV TZU SAEM SPELING BIKUZ TZU SPELING IZ DITURMIND BIE TZU SAUND. [With Phonemic English no words that sound differently can have the same spelling because the spelling is determined by the sound.]

FUNEEMIK INGXGLISH [Phonemic English] WUN-LETUR VAUXULZ [One-Letter Vowels]	
IF IT LUUKS LIEK [If It Looks Like]	**TZEN IT SAUNDZ LIEK** [Then It Sounds Like]
A	A
E	E
I	I
O	O
U	U

FUNEEMIK INGXGLISH [Phonemic English] TUE-LETUR VAUXULZ [Two-Letter Vowels]	
IF IT LUUKS LIEK [If It Looks Like]	**TZEN IT SAUNDZ LIEK** [Then It Sounds Like]
AE	AE
EE	EE
IE	IE
OE	OE
UE	UE
UU	UU

CHAPTER 10

So Many Meanings,
So Few Words

The Tilde (~) Tool

We provide the **tilde (~) tool** to help the author temporarily identify a word or phrase for which the author has a special meaning or has not yet determined a specific meaning. Once the author has determined a specific meaning, she/he can apply her/his own meaning or cite a dictionary definition using **AlphaNumeric (@#)** notation in the document. The Tilde Tool can be used with numeric notation to facilitate finding tilde words or phrases. If the author wishes, once meanings have been established, tilde words or phrases can be converted easily to footnotes or endnotes in the author's document.

Words That Are Spelled the Same and Pronounced the Same But Have Different Meanings

The problem of distinguishing different meanings among words that are spelled the same and pronounced the same is identical in both Phonemic English and Standard English. For example the Random House Webster unabridged dictionary contains more than 170 different meanings for the word "run". In non-consequential writings such as recreational novels different meanings for a given word do not cause serious problems and meaning can usually be derived from context. However, in substantive writings such as critical arguments slight differences in meaning for a given word can cause misinterpretations which can create misunderstandings that can lead to disagreements. Table 10-1 gives examples of our method of distinguishing different meanings among words that are spelled the same and pronounced the same:

Table 10-1. Examples of our method of distinguishing different meanings among words that are spelled the same and pronounced the same.

Spelled the same, PRONOUNCED the same, but different meanings:
Run~ a race. A home **run~**. ~ = Author's uncertain **meaning**.
RUN U RAES. U HOEM **RUN**. ~ = Author's uncertain **meaning**.
Run~1 a race. A home **run~2**. ~# = Author's uncertain **meaning** with numeric notation.
RUN~1 U RAES. U HOEM **RUN~2** ~# = Author's uncertain **meaning** with numeric notation.
Run2 a race. A home **run3**. Author's **meaning**.
RUN2 U RAES. U HOEM **RUN3** Author's **meaning**.
Run-v.6.a. a race. A home **run-n.6.** American Heritage Dictionary's **meaning**.
RUN-v.6.a. U RAES. U HOEM **RUN-n.6.** American Heritage Dictionary's **meaning**.

When using her/his own meanings with AlphaNumeric notation, the author should include with her/his document a glossary that provides the specific meanings of her/his AlphaNumeric words. When using a dictionary's (or other source's) meanings with AlphaNumeric notation, the author should include with her/his document a glossary that cites the specific dictionary (or other source) of each meaning. Note that the AlphaNumeric suffixes (AlphaNumeric prefixes can be used as well) are not pronounced when speaking or reading aloud.

Words That Are Spelled the Same but are Pronounced Differently and Have Different Meanings

Phonemic English automatically solves the problem of words that are spelled the same but are pronounced differently, because **Phonemic English words** that are **pronounced differently** are **spelled differently**. AlphaNumeric notation solves the problem of Standard English words that are spelled the same but are pronounced differently as shown in Table 10-2:

Table 10-2. AlphaNumeric notation solves the problem of Standard English words that are spelled the same but are pronounced differently.

Spelled the same, but PRONOUNCED differently, different meanings:
Read~ the book. He read~ the book. ~ = Author's uncertain meaning.
REED~ TZU BUUK. HEE RED~ TZU BUUK. ~ = Author's uncertain meaning.
Read~3 the book. He read~4 the book. ~# = Author's uncertain meaning with numeric notation.
REED~3 TZU BUUK. HEE RED~4 TZU BUUK. ~# = Author's uncertain meaning with numeric notation.
Read2 the book. He read3 (did read2) the book. Author's meaning.
REED2 TZU BUUK. HEE RED3 (DID REED2) TZU BUUK. Author's meaning.
Read-v.1. the book. He read-v.2. (did read-v.1.) the book. AHD's meaning.
REED-v.1. TZU BUUK. HEE RED-v.2. (DID REED-v.1.) TZU BUUK. AHD's meaning.

Note that the AlphaNumeric suffixes are not pronounced when speaking or reading aloud.

Words That Are Spelled Differently but are Pronounced the Same and Have Different Meanings

Phonemic English words that are pronounced the same are spelled the same. AlphaNumeric notation solves the problem of Phonemic English words that are spelled the same and the problem of Standard

English words that are pronounced the same but are spelled differently as shown in Table 10-3:

Table 10-3. AlphaNumeric notation solves the problem of Phonemic English words that are spelled the same and the problem of Standard English words that are pronounced the same but are spelled differently.

Spelled differently, PRONOUNCED the same, but different meanings:
Bob is **two~** years **too~** young **to~** vote. ~ = Author's uncertain **meaning**.
BOB IZ **TUE~** YEERZ **TUE~** YUNG **TUE~** VOET. ~ = Author's uncertain **meaning**.
Bob is **two~5** years **too~6** young **to~7** vote. ~# = Author's uncertain **meaning** with numeric notation.
BOB IZ **TUE~5** YEERZ **TUE~6** YUNG **TUE~7** VOET. ~# = Author's uncertain **meaning** with numeric notation.
Bob is **two2** years **too3** young **to4** vote. Author's **meaning**.
BOB IZ **TUE2** YEERZ **TUE3** YUNG **TUE4** VOET. Author's **meaning**.
Bob is **two-n.1.(adj.)** years **too-adv.2.** young **to-prep.15.a.** vote. AHD's **meaning**.
BOB IZ **TUE-n.1.(adj.)** YEERZ **TUE-adv.2.** YUNG **TUE-prep.15.a.** VOET. AHD's **meaning**.

Note that the AlphaNumeric suffixes are not pronounced when speaking or reading aloud.

CHAPTER 11

Making Sense

Syllables, Prefixes, and Suffixes

Syllables

Because the alphabet is limited to 26 characters, and the maximum number of characters that can make up a syllable is also limited, there can be only about 16,000 syllables. The number of meaningful syllables in USA English is far less.

We believe that the smallest **increment of meaning** is the **syllable** and that the meaning imparted by the syllable is qualified by adding prefixes, suffixes and additional syllables to complete the word. Prefixes and suffixes are syllables, too. A word by itself has little meaning, but when two words are formed into a phrase, more specific meaning emerges. For example, consider the word **like**:

like <== single syllable word
LIEK

add the prefix **un**:
                UN

unlike <== two syllable word with meaning significantly changed
UNLIEK

add the suffix **ly**:
LEE

unlikely <== three syllable word with meaning again changed
UNLIEKLEE

Two-word Phrases

Our highly qualified word still communicates little significant meaning. See how meaning is communicated by adding another word to form a two-word phrase:

**rain unlikely <==two-word phrase with significant meaning
RAEN UNLIEKLEE**

Words have **definitions; phrases** have **meaning**. Now we are beginning to **make sense!**

Word Order

The meaning of our two-word phrase changes again when we reverse the word order:

**unlikely rain <===two-word phrase with meaning changed
UNLIEKLEE RAEN**

Word order is crucial to meaning!

Prefixes

Table 11-1. The most common prefixes based on a count of prefixed words appearing in the *Word Frequency Book*.

The Most Common Prefixes			
Rank	Prefix	Meaning	%
1	un	not, opposite of	26
2	re	again	14
3	in, im, ir, ill	not	11
4	dis	not, opposite of	7
5	en, em	cause to	4
6	non	not	4
7	in, im	in or into	4
8	over	too much	3
9	mis	wrongly	3
10	sub	under	3
11	pre	before	3
12	inter	between, among	3
13	fore	before	3
14	de	opposite of	2
15	trans	across	2
16	super	above	1
17	semi	half	1
18	anti	against	1
19	mid	middle	1
20	under	too little	1
All other prefixes (@ 100) accounted for only 3% of the words.			

Table 11-1 shows the most common prefixes based on a count of prefixed words appearing in the *Word Frequency Book* (Carrol, Davies, and Richman, 1971).

Suffixes

Table 11-2. The most common suffixes based on a count of suffixed words appearing in the *Word Frequency Book*.

The Most Common Suffixes			
Rank	Suffix	Meaning	%
1	s, es	plurals	31
2	ed	past-tense verbs	20
3	ing	verb form/present participle	14
4	ly	characteristic of	7
5	er, or	person connected with	4
6	ion, tion, ation, ition	act, process	4
7	ible, able	can be done	2
8	al, ial	having characteristics of	1
9	y	chacterized by	1
10	ness	state of, condition of	1
11	ity, ty	state of	1
12	ment	action or process	1
13	ic	having characteristics of	1
14	ous, eous, ious	possessing the qualities of	1
15	en	made of	1
16	er	comparative	1
17	ive, ative, itive	adjective form of a noun	1
18	ful	full of	1
19	less	without	1
20	est	comparative	1
All other suffixes (@ 160) accounted for only 7% of the words.			

Table 11-2 shows the most common suffixes based on a count of suffixed words appearing in the *Word Frequency Book* (Carrol, Davies, and Richman, 1971).

CHAPTER 12

Putting It All Together

General

This material is provided as a prototype for development by parents, grandparents, and siblings who help learners with homework as well as for tutors, teachers, and others who wish to create lessons for assisting or teaching learners and tutors of USA English. We do not create or give lessons.

The introduction of this material to a USA English learner requires a tutor who is thoroughly trained in the concepts and application of its contents.

What to Do

1. Create a **phonemic environment**:

Surround USA English learners with phoneme sounds and our typeable phoneme symbols in all manners that make sense: papers, books, pictures, toys, music, games, visual/aural aids, etc. Be sure that all reading is **reading aloud**.

Help the learner to identify and match the phoneme sounds and our phoneme symbols. It is crucial for the learner to understand that there is only **one phoneme sound per phoneme symbol** and only **one phoneme symbol per phoneme sound**.

Help the learner name the numerals, letters of the alphabet and the phonemes.

Introduce the use of our Silent X Marker for separating odd syllables and adjacent vowels.

2.   Introduce word structure:

Help the learner identify phonemes, blends, syllables, words, and phrases.

Introduce the concept of decoding and, where useful, employing the names of the phonemes to sound out words.

3.   Evaluate the learner's hearing, speech, and vision:

Employ the SpeechTest of Appendix I.

4.   Introduce the concept of "SeeSayMean" per Chapter 10:

Words that are spelled the same and pronounced the same but have different meanings.

Words that are spelled the same but pronounced differently and have different meanings.

Words that are spelled differently but pronounced the same and have different meanings.

5.   Introduce the use of the **talking dictionary**:

Help the learner lookup meanings of words.

Create word lists and show the learner how to create word lists and to **repeat aloud** all pronunciations.

Drill on weak pronunciations and introduce additional words containing the phonemes the learner might be having difficulty with.

6. Train the learner in the use of the **TwoLine Method**:

    The TwoLine Method **cements** the **bond** between Phonemic English and Standard English. This method is probably the most useful tool for the learner of USA English reading.
    Be sure the learner **pronounces** each word **aloud** and refers to a **talking dictionary** for the pronunciation and meaning of each word.

7. Introduce the learner to the concept of meaning, how words are changed by adding suffixes and prefixes, and how meaning changes with changes in word order.

8. Provide the learner practice exercises in speaking and reading (remember, reading is **reading alo**ud).

    Prototype drill materials including nursery rhymes, cartoons, and Lincoln's Gettysburg Address are provided in Appendix II.

CHAPTER 13

Other Possibilities

Avoid Irregular Verbs

A major problem in the teaching of USA English, particurly in the teaching of USA English as a second language, is the problem of irregular verbs. Nearly all, if not all, USA English verbs are irregular. Without even taking into account the absurd rules for tense, such a large number of irregular verbs creates another nightmare for USA English learners. The **conjugation** of each USA English verb **must be memorize**d. We propose teaching "KidsVerbs" first (remember, we are talking about communication), then later introducing "SchoolVerbs". KidsVerbs combine the tenses (not the conjugation) of the verb "do" with all other USA English verbs as shown in Table 13-1:

Table 13-1. Regular verb conjugation using the verb do.

	Verb:	Tense:	Conjugation:		
SchoolVerb Singular:	to do	Present Past Future	I do I did I will do	you do you did you will do	he/she/it does he/she/it did he/she/it will do
SchoolVerb Plural:	to do	Present Past Future	we do we did we will do	you do you did you will do	they do they did they will do

	Verb:	Tense:	Conjugation:		
KidsVerb Singular:	to do	Present Past Future	I do I did I will do	you do you did you will do	he/she/it do he/she/it did he/she/it will do
KidsVerb Plural:	to do	Present Past Future	we do we did we will do	you do you did you will do	they do they did they will do
SchoolVerb Singular:	to be	Present Past Future	I am I was I will be	you are you were you will be	he/she/it is he/she/it was he/she/it will be
SchoolVerb Plural:	to be	Present Past Future	we are we were we will be	you are you were you will be	they are they were they will be
KidsVerb Singular:	to be	Present Past Future	(do) not pronounced I (do) be I did be I will (do) be	(do) not pronounced you (do) be you did be you will (do) be	(do) not pronounced he/she/it (do) be he/she/it did be he/she/it will (do) be
KidsVerb Plural:	to be	Present Past Future	(do) not pronounced we (do) be we did be we will (do) be	(do) not pronounced you (do) be you did be you will (do) be	(do) not pronounced they (do) be they did be they will (do) be
SchoolVerb Singular:	to bake	Present Past Future	I bake I baked I will bake	you bake you baked you will bake	he/she/it bakes he/she/it baked he/she/it will bake
SchoolVerb Plural:	to bake	Present Past Future	we bake we baked we will bake	you bake you baked you will bake	they bake they baked they will bake
KidsVerb Singular:	to bake	Present Past Future	(do) not pronounced I (do) bake I did bake I will (do) bake	(do) not pronounced you (do) bake you did bake you will (do) bake	(do) not pronounced he/she/it (do) bake he/she/it did bake he/she/it will (do) bake
KidsVerb Plural:	to bake	Present Past Future	(do) not pronounced we (do) bake we did bake we will (do) bake	(do) not pronounced you (do) bake you did bake you will (do) bake	(do) not pronounced they (do) bake they did bake they will (do) bake
SchoolVerb Singular:	to make	Present Past Future	I make I made I will make	you make you made you will make	he/she/it makes he/she/it made he/she/it will make

	Verb:	Tense:	Conjugation:		
SchoolVerb Plural:	to make	Present Past Future	we make we made we will make	you make you made you will make	they make they made they will make
KidsVerb Singular:	to make	Present Past Future	(do) not pronounced I (do) make I did make I will (do) make	(do) not pronounced you (do) make you did make you will (do) make	(do) not pronounced he/she/it (do) make he/she/it did make he/she/it will (do) make
KidsVerb Plural:	to make	Present Past Future	(do) not pronounced we (do) make we did make we will (do) make	(do) not pronounced you (do) make you did make you will (do) make	(do) not pronounced they (do) make they did make they will (do) make
SchoolVerb Singular:	to take	Present Past Future	I take I took I will take	you take you took you will take	he/she/it takes he/she/it took he/she/it will take
SchoolVerb Plural:	to take	Present Past Future	we take we took we will take	you take you took you will take	they take they took they will take
KidsVerb Singular:	to take	Present Past Future	(do) not pronounced I (do) take I did take I will (do) take	(do) not pronounced you (do) take you did take you will (do) take	(do) not pronounced he/she/it (do) take he/she/it did take he/she/it will (do) take
KidsVerb Plural:	to take	Present Past Future	(do) not pronounced we (do) take we did take we will (do) take	(do) not pronounced you (do) take you did take you will (do) take	(do) not pronounced they (do) take they did take they will (do) take

Table 13-1. KidsVerbs combine the tenses (not the conjugation) of the verb "do" with all other USA English verbs to regularize the irregular verbs of USA English.

After Reading Comes Comprehension

USA English learners are not provided adequate tools to comprehend fully what they are reading. **Comprehension is not memorization.** From birth on, a child learns by applying her/his senses to everything she/he encounters in her/his environment. This process is **fundamental studying** and is a phenomenon of the **brain**. When a child encounters reading, her/his natural studying process (**brain**) must be augmented by learning other studying processes (**mind**). By the time a person enters college she/he might augment studying substantive text by using marks such as underlining, circling, and highlighting to identify important passages as well as making several forms of margin notes. This augmentation process is learned on an individual basis; it is seldom taught. Combined with the lack of teaching is the lack on the part of authors, writers, and editors to provide clues to the identification of important passages in substantive text. The learner is expected to comprehend what she/he is reading without training, assistance, or other support.

We take the position that comprehension is not solely the responsibility of the reader; **comprehension** is also the **responsibility of the writer**. If I can't make sense of what you wrote, it is your fault; if you can't make sense of what I wrote, it is my fault. With the rapid development of internet publishing as well as electronic book technology, publishers must adopt new techniques to allow authors to make sense and to allow readers to comprehend. The most powerful tool available to help the writer make sense is hypertext. Hypertext alone is not sufficient. We provide additional tools to assist both writers and readers to make sense in substantive matters.

Tools to Help the Reader

1. Set the scope: Mark both the beginning and the end of the selection to be studied.

2. Scan (quickly look over) the entire selection, marking anything that stands out or looks difficult to understand.

3. Read (aloud, if possible; say to yourself, if reading aloud is not possible) a connected passage of the selection.

4. Silently read the same passage again and mark keywords or short keyphrases. Since not all keywords or keyphrases are equally important, rank them in order of relative importance by giving each ranking a different mark. Draw a line joining keywords or keyphrases that make a connection.

5. Read the same passage again to determine whether you understand what the author is saying.

6. If you do not understand or if you need to clarify what the author is saying, rewrite the passage in a way that makes sense to you.

7. Mark the passage you have rewritten as in item 4. above using any combination of pencil; pen; colored pencils; colored pens; a four-colored pen; and felt-tipped, colored highlighters. Employ a sensible, consistent method of marking such as shown in Table 13-2:

Table 13-2. Our suggested markings for readers of text on paper.

Marker	Key Words	Key Phrases	Emphasised Words or Phrases	Connections
Pencil or Pen	Underline	Circle	Underline and Circle	Line Between Circled Words or Phrases

Marker	Key Words	Key Phrases	Emphasised Words or Phrases	Connections
Colored Pencils or Pens	Circle in Green	Circle in Blue	Underline and Circle in Green	Line Between Circled Words or Phrases
Colored Highlighter	Yellow	Green	Blue	Line Between Highlighted and Circled Words or Phrases

Use any combination of markers and colors you want. Be consistent in their use. Augment these marks with margin notes and any other marks you choose.

Tools to Help the Writer

1. Select and read aloud a portion of your text, marking anything that stands out or looks difficult to understand.

2. Read the same passage again and mark keywords or short keyphrases. Since not all keywords or keyphrases are equally important, rank them in order of relative importance by giving each ranking a different mark. Draw a line joining keywords or keyphrases that make a connection.

3. If you need to clarify what you are saying, rewrite the passage in a way that makes sense to you.

4. Where applicable use the tools of "SeeSayMean" per Chapter 9.

5. Mark the passage you have rewritten using any combination of pencil; pen; colored pencils; colored pens; a four-colored pen; and felt-tipped, colored highlighters. Employ a sensible, consistent method of marking such as shown in Table 13-3:

Table 13-3. Our suggested markings for writers of text on paper.

Marker	Key Words	Key Phrases	Emphasised Words or Phrases	Connections
Pencil or Pen	Underline	Circle	Underline and Circle	Line Between Circled Words or Phrases
Colored Pencils or Pens	Circle in Green	Circle in Blue	Underline and Circle in Green	Line Between Circled Words or Phrases
Colored Highlighter	Yellow	Green	Blue	Line Between Highlighted and Circled Words or Phrases

Use any combination of markers and colors you want. Be consistent in their use. Augment these marks with margin notes and any other marks you choose.

CHAPTER 14

Hope for the Future

Our Prediction

We predict that the increasing difficulty with accompanying lack of success that schools face in teaching USA English reading along with the rapid development and widespread use of personal computers will force adoption, first in some states then nationwide, of a standardized, consistent, sensible system of typeable phoneme symbols.

Our Hope

The nineteenth-century German philosopher Arthur Schopenhauer said: "All truth passes through three stages. First, it is ridiculed. Second, it is violently opposed. Third, it is accepted as being self-evident."

The idea of Phonemic English, an idea whose time has come, currently suffers from the first stage—it is just not taken seriously. As its general applicability to the learning of English and its broad usefulness as a meta-language become increasingly apparent, the concept of Phonemic English begins to challenge current methods and is becoming a threat to established educators and researchers alike, thus moving to Schopenhauer's second stage.

Our typeable phoneme symbols and other tools and methods are the ideal solution for adoption by all entities teaching USA English. As of this writing, our tools and methods are relatively untried. It is our hope that a graduate program or other similar institution will challenge the material provided here, test our tools and methods under reliable, controlled conditions, and report its findings in the public literature.

It would be of great advantage to teachers and publishers as well as learning-products manufacturers to enhance their programs by integrating our tools and methods into their current and ongoing efforts and products.

APPENDIX I

Evaluate the Learner's Hearing, Speech, and Vision

Our SpeechTest

Our SpeechTest is not intended to be a self-test. It is intended to be administered by the learner's helper (parent, grandparent, sibling, tutor, teacher). The learner's helper must pass the test first by correcting any difficulties encountered in taking the test. The test is administered by having the learner pronounce each word after hearing the dictionary's pronunciation of the word. The helper has the learner repeat any difficult pronunciations and suggests other words containing the difficult phoneme sound. Once the learner is proficient in pronunciation, the helper covers the Standard English line and has the learner pronounce each word in the Phonemic English line without using the dictionary. When the learner is proficient in pronouncing the Phonemic English line without the dictionary, the helper covers the Phonemic English line and has the learner pronounce each word in the Standard English line without using the dictionary.

Our SpeechTest allows the learner to hear, say and see keywords that demonstrate the phoneme sounds and symbols of USA English. Using the TwoLine Method, the keywords are listed in groups. Except for the Consonant Blends and Other Words Groups, the groups are arranged in order of relative difficulty, easiest to most difficult as shown below.

(18) One-Letter Consonants

bad	dad	fad	got	hot	jot	<== Standard English
BAD	DAD	FAD	GOT	HOT	JOT	<== Phonemic English
kit	lit	met	not	pot	rot	
KIT	LIT	MET	NOT	POT	ROT	
sat	tat	vat	wet	yet	zap	
SAT	TAT	VAT	WET	YET	ZAP	

(7) Two-Letter Consonants

chin	shin	thin	then\	when	azure\	sing
CHIN	SHIN	THIN	TZEN	WHEN	AZHUR	SING

(5) One-Letter Vowels

pap	pep	pip	pop	pup
PAP	PEP	PIP	POP	PUP

(6) Two-Letter Vowels

take\	teeth	tie	toe	true	took\	\ <== keywords do not match
TAEK	TEETH	TIE	TOE	TRUE	TUUK	

Vowel Blends

shout\	boil
SHAUT	BOIL

Consonant Blends

blend	blends\	brand	burnt	close\	flake\	fry\
BLEND	BLENDZ	BRAND	BURNT	KLOEZ	FLAEK	FRIE

glad	grate\	hurts	slow\	snow\	special\	trash
GLAD	GRAET	HURTS	SLOE	SNOE	SPESHUL	TRASH

Other Words

coerce\	dare\	defer\	differ\
KOEXURS	DAR	DIXFUR	DIFXUR

father\	order\	pier\	urge\
FOXTZUR	OERXDUR	PEER	URJ

APPENDIX II

Prototype Drill Materials

Common Words

The 150 Most Frequent Words
(In Order of Frequency)

Lower case = Standard English, ALL CAPS = Phonemic English:
the = TZU (or TZEE) (Options)
of = UV
and = AND
a = A (or AE or U)
to = TUE (or TU)

in = IN
is = IZ
you = YUE
that = TZAT
it = IT

he = HEE
for = FOER
was = WUZ
on = ON
are = OR

but = BUT
what = WHOT (or WHUT)
all = ALL
were = WUR
when – WHEN

we = WEE
there = TZAR
can = KAN
an = AN
your = YUUR (or YOER or YUR)

which = WHICH
their = TZAR
said = SED
if = IF
do = DUE

into = INXTUE
has = HAZ
more = MOER
her = HUR
two = TUE

like = LIEK
him = HIM
see = SEE
time = TIEM
could = KUUD

no = NOE
make = MAEK
than = TZAN
first = FURST
been = BIN

long = LONG
little = LITXUL
very = VERXEE
after = AFXTUR
words = WURDZ

called = KOLD
just = JUST
where = WHAR
most = MOEST
know = NOE

get = GET
through = THRUE
back = BAK
much = MUCH
before = BIXFOER

also = OLXSOE
around = UXRAUND
another = UXNUTZXUR
came = KAEM
come = KUM

work = WURK
three = THREE
word = WURD
must = MUST
because = BIXKOZ

does = DUZ
part = PORT
even = EEXVUN
place = PLAES
well = WEL

as = AZ
with = WITH
his = HIZ
they = TZAE
at = AT

be = BEE
this = TZIS
from = FRUM
I = IE
have = HAV

or = OER (or UR)
by = BIE
one = WUN
had = HAD
not = NOT

will = WIL
each = EECH
about = UXBAUT
how = HAU
up = UP

out = AUT
them = TZEM
then = TZEN
she = SHEE
many = MENXEE

some = SUM
so = SOE
these = TZEEZ
would = WUUD
other = UTZXUR

its = ITZ
who = WHUE
now = NAU
people = PEEXPUL
my = MIE

made = MAED
over = OEXVUR
did = DID
down = DAUN
only = OENXLEE

way = WAE
find = FIEND
use = YUEZ (or YUES)
may = MAE
water = WOXTUR

go = GOE
good = GUUD
new = NUE
write = RIET
our = AUR

used = YUEZD
me = MEE
man = MAN
too = TUE
any = ENXEE

day = DAE
same = SAEM
right = RIET
look = LUUK
think = THINK

such = SUCH
here = HEER
take = TAEK
why = WHIE
things = THINGZ

help = HELP
put = PUUT
years = YEERZ
different = DIFXURXUNT (or DIFXRUNT)
away = UXWAE

again = UXGEN
off = OF
went = WENT
old = OELD
number = NUMXBUR

Source: The American Heritage Word Frequency Book by John B. Carroll, Peter Davies, and Barry Richman (Houghton Mifflin, 1971, ISBN 0-395-13570-2).

Nursery Rhymes

(2) Mother Goose Nursery Rhymes...
Do-Read aloud

> **Top Rows: Standard English/ MIND-"knows"**
> **Bottom Rows: Phonemic English/BRAIN-"knows"**

Jack Sprat could eat no fat.
JAK SPRAT KUUD EET NOE FAT.

His wife could eat no lean.
HIZ WIEF KUUD EET NOE LEEN.

And so between them both, you see,
AND SOE BIXTWEEN TZEM BOETH, YUE SEE,

They licked the platter clean.
TZAE LIKT TZU PLATXUR KLEEN.

Old King Cole was a merry old soul,
OELD KING KOEL WOZ U MERXEE OELD SOEL,

And a merry old soul was he.
AND U MERXEE OELD SOEL WOZ HEE.

He called for his pipe,
HEE KOLD FOER HIZ PIEP,

And he called for his bowl,
AND HEE KOLD FOER HIZ BOEL,

And he called for his fiddlers three.
AND HEE KOLD FOER HIZ FIDXLURZ THREE.

Lincoln's Gettysburg Address

Top Rows: Standard English/ *MIND*-"knows"
Bottom Rows: Phonemic English/*BRAIN*-"knows"
    SEE-silently, and <u>rapidly</u> (*scanning*), Top-Row;
    then SAY-aloud, and <u>slowly</u>, Bottom-Row...

Four score and seven years ago our fathers
FOER SKOER AND SEVUN YEERZ UGOE AUR FOTZURZ

brought forth on this continent a new nation,
BROT FOERTH ON TZIS KONTUNUNT U NUENAESHUN,

conceived in liberty and dedicated to the
KONSEEVD IN LIBURTEE AND DEDIKAETID TUE TZU

proposition that all men are created equal.
PROPUZISHUN TZAT OL MEN OR KREEXAETID EEKWUL.

Now we are engaged in a great civil war,
NAU WEE OR ENGAEJD IN U GRAET SIVIL WOER,

testing whether that nation or any nation so
TESTING WHETZER TZAT NAESHUN OER ENEE NAESHUN SOE

conceived and so dedicated can long endure.
KUNSEEVD AND SOE DEDIKAETID KAN LONG ENDUER.

We are met on a great battlefield of that war.
WEE OR MET ON U GRAET BATULFEELD UV TZAT WOER.

We have come to dedicate a portion of that field,
WEE HAV KUM TUE DEDIKAET U POERSHUN UV TZAT FEELD,

as a final resting place for those who here
AZ U FIENUL RESTING PLAES FOER TZOEZ HUE HEER

gave their lives that that nation might live.
GAEV TZAR LIEVS TZAT TZAT NAESHUN MIET LIV.

It is altogether fitting and proper
IT IZ OLTUGETZUR FITING AND PROPUR

that we should do this.
TZAT WEE SHUUD DUE TZIS.

But, in a larger sense, we can not dedicate-
BUT, IN U LORJUR SENS, WEE KAN NOT DEDIKAET-

we can not consecrate-
WEE KAN NOT KONSIKRAET-

we can not hallow- this ground.
WEE KAN NOT HALOE- TZIS GRAUND.

The brave men, living and dead, who struggled here,
TZU BRAEV MEN, LIVING AND DED, HUE STRUGULD HEER,

have consecrated it, far above our
HAV KONSIKRAETID IT, FOR UBUV AUR

poor power to add or detract.
PUUR PAUXUR TUE AD OER DITRAKT.

The world will little note, nor long remember,
TZU WURLD WIL LITUL NOET, NOER LONG RIMEMBUR,

what we say here, but it can not
WHOT WEE SAE HEER, BUT IT KAN NOT

forget what they did here.
FURGET WHOT TZAE DID HEER.

It is for us the living, rather,
IT IZ FOER US TZU LIVING, RATZUR,

to be dedicated here to the unfinished work
TUE BEE DEDIKAETUD HEER TUE TZU UNFINISHT WURK

which they who fought here
WHICH TZAE HUE FOT HEER

have thus far so nobly advanced.
HAV TZUS FOR SOE NOEBLEE ADVANST.

It is rather for us to be dedicated to
IT IZ RATZUR FOER US TUE BEE DEDIKAETUD TUE

the great task remaining before us-
TZU GRAET TASK RIMAENING BIFOER US-

that from these dead we take increased devotion
TZAT FRUM TZEEZ DED WEE TAEK INKREEST DIVOESHUN

to that cause for which they gave
TUE TZAT KOZ FOER WHICH TZAE GAEV

the last full measure of devotion-
TZU LAST FUUL MEZHUR UV DIVOESHUN-

that we here highly resolve that these dead
TZAT WEE HEER HIELEE RIZOLV TZAT TZEEZ DED

shall not have died in vain-
SHAL NOT HAV DIED IN VAEN-

that this nation, under God,
TZAT TZIS NAESHUN, UNDUR GOD,

shall have a new birth of freedom-
SHAL HAV U NUE BURTH UV FREEDUM-

and that government of the people,
AND TZAT GUVURNMUNT UV TZU PEEPUL,

by the people, for the people,
BIE TZU PEEPUL, FOER TZU PEEPUL,

shall not perish from the earth.
SHAL NOT PERISH FRUM TZU URTH.

APPENDIX III

Using Phoneme Names for Sounding Out Words

The names of the phonemes can be quite helpful for sounding out words that are difficult to pronounce. Here's how it is done:

First, type the word in Phonemic English:

GET

Second, decode the word:

G.E.T

Third, type the names of the phonemes under the decoded word:

G. E. T
Gu.Ek.Tu

Fourth, as you read the names aloud, drop the suffixes (u & k) one-by-one:

Gu.Ek.Tu

G.Ek.Tu

G.E.Tu

G.E.T

In most cases pronunciation difficulties are caused by vowel sounds. It may not be necessary to type both the consonant and vowel phoneme names under the decoded word in order to sound out the word. Typing the vowel phoneme names only might be all that is needed. For example try the word continent:

First, type the word in Phonemic English:

KONTUNUNT

Second, decode the word to separate phonemes only:

K.O.N.T.U.N.U.N.T

Third, type the names of the vowel phonemes under the decoded word:

K.O.N.T.U.N.U.N.T
Ok   Uk Uk

Fourth, drilling on the names of the vowel phonemes while reading the decoded word aloud will reinforce pronunciation of the vowel phoneme sounds.

In the case of longer or more complicated words, treat each syllable as a separate word. Consider the word extraordinary, for example:

First, type the word in Phonemic English:

IKSTROERDUNEREE

Second, decode the word to separate syllables only:

IK'STROER'DUN'ER'EE

Third, decode each syllable to separate phonemes only:

I.K S.T.R.OE.R D.U.N E.R EE

Fourth, type the names of the vowel phonemes under each decoded syllable:

I.K S.T.R.OE.R D.U.N E.R EE
Ik   OEk   Uk Ek EEk

Fifth, drilling on the names of the vowel phonemes while reading each decoded syllable aloud will reinforce pronunciation of the vowel phoneme sounds.

Sixth, reconstruct the word by reading aloud all the syllables in succession as if they made up a phrase:

IK STROER DUN ER EE

Finally, read aloud the reconstructed word:

IKSTROERDUNEREE

The Silent X Marker can be helpful in showing the syllable separations:

IKXSTROERXDUNXERXEE

ACKNOWLEDGEMENTS

I was unaware, as I believe are most American English learners, of the concept of phonemes until I met Kermit W. (Kert) Dees who was then about 87 years old. In our first conversation I learned that he had created his own website and that he needed a helper. I volunteered to be his helper if, in exchange, he would teach me how to write web pages. I soon learned that he knew a great deal about phonemes and almost nothing about web pages, so I took a beginner's course in HTML and Kert began the arduous task of teaching me about phonemes, including the phoneme symbols, the names of the phonemes, the Silent-X marker, the Tilde Tool and the Speech Test.

Kert soon introduced me to another helper, David M. Larson, who had contributed to Kert's work and who continued for a short period to contribute primarily computer assistance to this work.

Later Kert met and introduced me to Kenneth W. Carter who had shown considerable interest in Kert's work. Ken contributed materially to this work including writing the Foreword and voice-recording some of the words.

Later still I recruited Paul Ulbrich and Guadalupe de la Concha to join our team and participate in our presentations, discussions and attempts to organize and make use of the work Kert had begun. Both contributed materially to this effort.

REFERENCES

Reading Organizations

National Right to Read Foundation - https://right2readfoundation.org/
National Institute for Literacy - https://www.federalregister.gov/agencies/
    national-institute-for-literacy
International Reading Association - https://study.com/

Phonemic Awareness

Phoneme Awareness - http://reading.uoregon.edu/
Phonemic Awareness Instruction - https://www.readandspell.com/us/
    teaching-phonemic-awareness
K-2 Phonemic Awareness Instruction - http://reading.uoregon.edu/

Learning Materials

Super Duper Publications - https://www.superduperinc.com/

Other Systems

Truespel - https://www.truespel.com/phonemes/

BIBLIOGRAPHY

Origin of speech - Wikipedia, the Free Encyclopedia, http://en.wikipedia.org/wiki/Origin_of_speech

Peter Whitmore - Phonetic spellings would help learners of English, https://www.nzherald.co.nz/nz/peter-whitmore-phonetic-spellings-would-help-learners-of-english/SUO7Q3YDYKS4XQVSIHBYVGOW3E/

Schwa (video) - https://www.merriam-webster.com/video/schwa

SourceWire.com - Can English spelling standards be improved with better teaching?, http://www.sourcewire.com/news/74265/crystal-clear-or-clear-as-a-bell-english-spelling-standards

The English Spelling Society - Irregularities of English spelling, http://spellingsociety.org/irregularities-of-english-spelling#/page/1

The English Spelling Society - What Is Wrong With English Spelling?, http://www.spellingsociety.org/